Prehistoric Creatures

Dinosaur Skeletons and Skulls

Joanne Mattern

Reading consultant: Susan Nations, M.Ed., author/literacy coach/consultant

WR WEEKLY READER
EARLY LEARNING LIBRARY

Please visit our web site at: www.earlyliteracy.cc
For a free color catalog describing Weekly Reader® Early Learning Library's
list of high-quality books, call 1-877-445-5824 (USA) or 1-800-387-3178 (Canada).
Weekly Reader® Early Learning Library's fax: (414) 336-0164.

Library of Congress Cataloging-in-Publication Data

Mattern, Joanne, 1963-
    Dinosaur skeletons and skulls / Joanne Mattern.
      p. cm. — (Prehistoric creatures)
    Includes bibliographical references and index.
    ISBN 0-8368-4897-7 (lib. bdg.)
    ISBN 0-8368-4904-3 (softcover)
    1. Dinosaur—Juvenile literature. I. Title. II. Series.
  QE861.5.M346   2005
  567.9—dc22   2005042872

This edition first published in 2006 by
Weekly Reader® Early Learning Library
A Member of the WRC Media Family of Companies
330 West Olive Street, Suite 100
Milwaukee, WI 53212 USA

Copyright © 2006 by Weekly Reader® Early Learning Library

Managing editor: Valerie J. Weber
Art direction and design: Tammy West

Illustrations: John Alston, Lisa Alderson, Dougal Dixon, Simon Mendez, Luis Rey

Printed in the United States of America

1 2 3 4 5 6 7 8 9 09 08 07 06 05

Long before there were people there were dinosaurs and other prehistoric creatures.

They roamed lands around the world. These creatures came in many shapes and sizes. Some had claws or sharp teeth. Others had spikes, long tails, or wings.

In this book, you will read about skeletons and skulls. Look for a label with the creature's name. You will also see how to say its name.

Archelon
(ARK-uh-lahn)

A Dinosaur's Body

Dinosaurs and other prehistoric creatures lived and died millions of years ago. How can scientists learn what these animals looked like? They study fossils of their skeletons. These fossils can tell them many things.

Fossils show that this dinosaur walked on long, strong back legs. It held its short front legs straight out. A long tail helped the dinosaur balance.

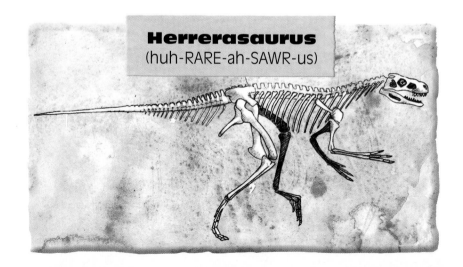

Herrerasaurus
(huh-RARE-ah-SAWR-us)

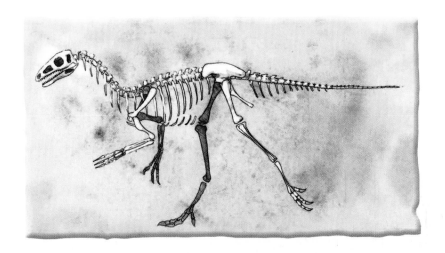

Nqwebasaurus
(n-KWE-bah-SAWR-us)

Stomach Stones

When scientists found this dinosaur's fossils, they also found gizzard stones. The dinosaur swallowed these stones to help it grind up food in its stomach. It ate small mammals, lizards, and insects.

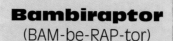

Built Like a Bird?

For years, people thought many dinosaurs were built like birds. During the 1990s, scientists found a skeleton that showed this was true. Its bones were just like a bird's.

A Speedy Runner

This dinosaur's skeleton also looks like a bird's. Its leg bones were a lot like an ostrich's leg bones. Scientists believe that this dinosaur's legs were light. Light legs helped it run very fast.

Ornithomimus
(or-NITH-oh-MIME-us)

Not Just Bones!

Most fossils are just bones. Scientists got a nice surprise when they found this fossil in the 1990s. The fossil also showed the animal's **lungs** and **intestines**. Lungs help an animal breathe. Intestines help it turn its food into energy. This animal's skeleton showed that it could breathe well when it ran.

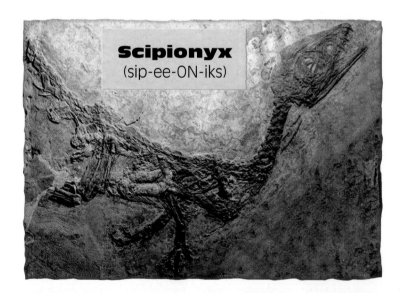

Scipionyx
(sip-ee-ON-iks)

In the Swim

This creature's skeleton shows that its body was built for swimming. It had a flat tail. Its legs pushed the creature through the water. This creature was a lizard about as long as a fox.

Aigialosaur
(ah-GEE-ah-lah-SAWR)

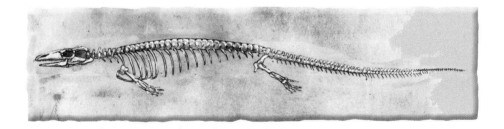

Life Underwater

This prehistoric reptile swam deep under the water. With its big, heavy bones, it could sink down to feed on the sea bottom. Its big rib cage held large lungs, so it could hold its breath for a long time. Its big lungs also helped it float.

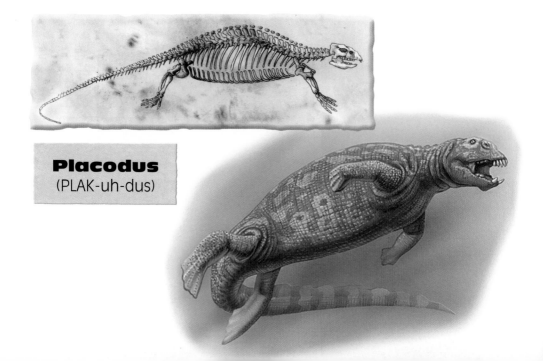

Placodus
(PLAK-uh-dus)

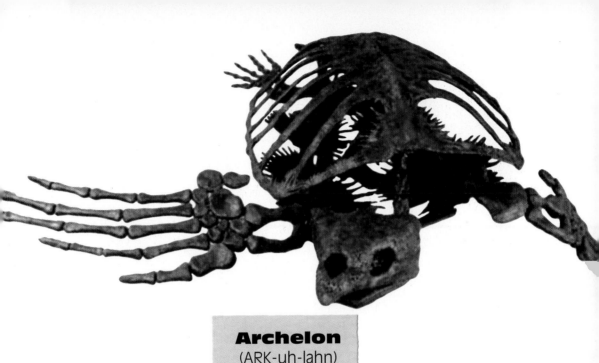

Archelon
(ARK-uh-lahn)

Big and Bony

This is the skeleton of the biggest turtle that ever lived. It grew to be longer than a rowboat! Its shell was made of bone covered by tough skin. This prehistoric turtle's jaws were not very strong. It probably ate soft foods, such as jellyfish.

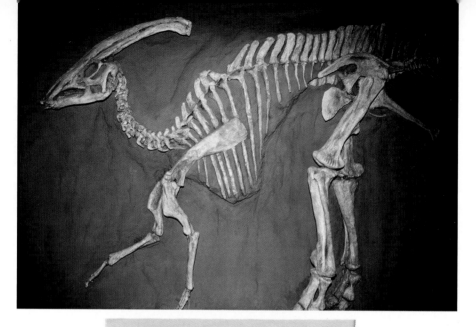

Parasaurolophus
(PAR-ah-SAW-ruh-LOH-fus)

Crest Bones

Some dinosaurs had long **crests** on top of their heads. Crests are long spikes on a dinosaur's head. Most crests were made of hollow bones. They were attached to the creature's skull. These dinosaurs may have used their crests to call loudly to each other.

Meat Eaters and Plant Eaters

A dinosaur's skull can tell us what kind of food it ate. The dinosaur on the left ate plants. Most of its teeth were the same size. They were jagged along the edges. The points helped the dinosaur shred leaves.

The dinosaur on the right had sharp, strong teeth. Teeth shaped like spikes helped it tear meat from bones.

Plateosaurus
(PLAT-ee-oh-SAWR-us)

Tyrannosaurus
(tie-RAN-oh-SAWR-us)

Boneheads

Skulls came in all sizes and shapes. One group of dinosaurs had high heads made of thick bone. This dinosaur was the smallest of these boneheads. It was probably only the size of a rabbit. It does have the longest name of any dinosaur, however!

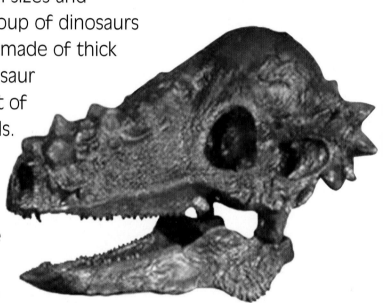

Micropachycephalosaurus
(MY-croe-PAK-ee-SEF-ah-loe-SAWR-us)

Hypsilophodon
(hip-seh-LOFF-oh-don)

Beaks and Teeth

This skull shows that the dinosaur had a beak like a bird's on the front of its head. It used this beak to pull up plants to eat. Its teeth are shaped for grinding and chopping. This skull also has holes at the side of its jaws. Cheek pouches that held food might have been there.

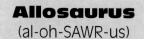

Allosaurus
(al-oh-SAWR-us)

Super Size!

This dinosaur's skull was about as long
as a bobcat. It had more than seventy
teeth in its mouth! Its lower jaw had hinges.
They could move sideways so this dinosaur could
stretch its mouth around large chunks of meat.

Long Jaws

This dinosaur's skull also held long jaws full of sharp teeth. This creature could catch big fish, squid, and giant reptiles in the ocean. The holes on top of its skulls were small nostrils. It probably breathed through its mouth when it came to the surface.

Pliosaur
(PLY-oh-SAWR)

Monster Skull

This dinosaur's skull was huge compared to the human skull next to it. Strong teeth curved like a shark's filled its big mouth. Its teeth were as long as a toothbrush! This dinosaur grew bigger than Tyrannosaurus rex!

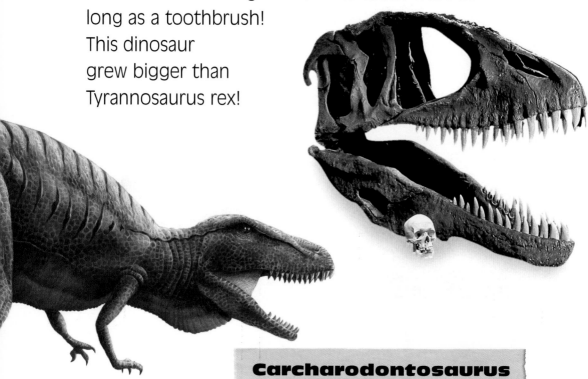

Carcharodontosaurus
(kahr-KAR-o-dont-o-SAWR-us)

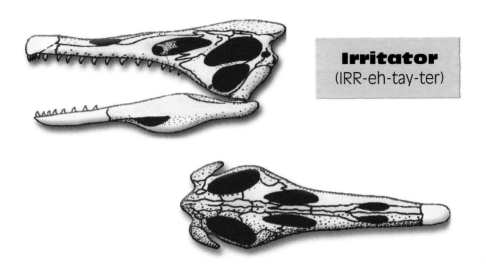

Fooled You!

Some dinosaur skulls are not what they seem.
In the 1990s, someone found this dinosaur's big
skull and sold it to a museum. The people at the
museum got a surprise, however. The person who
found the skull had added pieces of bone to it to
make it look bigger. Can you see from its name
how the museum people felt?

Not a Dinosaur

Not all prehistoric creatures were dinosaurs. This creature had fur like a mammal, but it was a reptile. It may have used its huge skull to butt other animals. It lived even before the dinosaurs did.

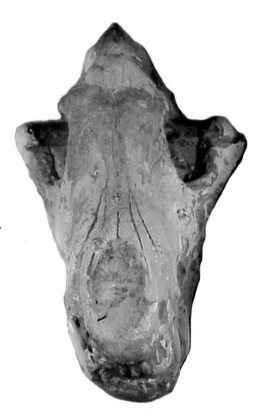

Moschops
(mus-KOPS)

Bony Bird

The skeleton of this flying reptile was found in rocks made of limestone. Scientists could see the creature's bones and the marks from its wings. Like all fossils, the skull and skeleton of this dinosaur help scientists learn what life was like millions of years ago.

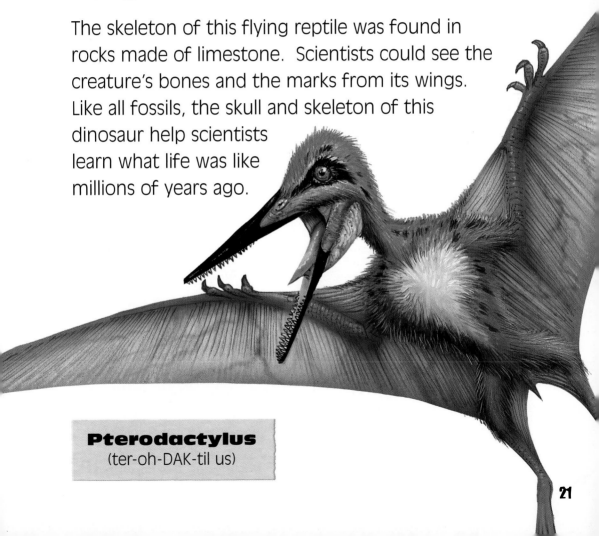

Pterodactylus
(ter-oh-DAK-til us)

Glossary

balance — to keep steady

fossils — remains of an animal or plant that lived millions of years ago

hinges — joints that move

limestone — rock formed from the remains of shells

lungs — organs inside the chest that are used to breathe

mammal — a warm-blooded animal with a backbone

nostrils — openings in the skull used to smell and as part of taste

prehistoric — living in times before written history

reptile — a cold-blooded animal with skin covered in scales or bony plates like armor

skeletons — bones that support and protect the body

skull — the bones of the head that protect the brain

For More Information

Books

Allosaurus. Exploring Dinosaurs (series). Susan Gray
   (Child's World)

Dinosaur Skeletons: A Pop-Up Book John Mallam (Yearling)

Parasaurolophus Daniel Cohen (Bridgestone Books)

Sea Turtles: Past and Present. Prehistoric Animals and
   Their Modern-Day Relatives (series). Marianne Johnston
   (PowerKids Press)

Web Sites

Zoom Dinosaurs
*www.enchantedlearning.com/subjects/dinosaurs/
   info/a.shtml*
Fact sheets on hundreds of dinosaurs, as well as a
dinosaur dictionary

Index

birds 6, 7, 15
bones 6, 7, 8, 10, 11, 12, 14, 19, 21
cheek pouches 15
crests 12
food 5, 8, 13, 15
fossils 4, 5, 8, 21
fur 20
gizzard 5
hinges 16
intestines 8
jaws 11, 16, 17
legs 4, 7, 9
limestone 21
lizards 5, 9
lungs 8, 10
mammals 5, 20
meat 13, 16
nostrils 17
plants 13, 15
Pterodactylus 21
reptiles 10, 17, 20, 21
rib cage 10
skin 11
swimming 9, 10
tails 4, 9
teeth 13, 15, 16, 17, 18
turtle 11
Tyrannosaurus 13, 18
wings 21

About the Author

Joanne Mattern is the author of more than 130 books for children. Her favorite subjects are animals, history, sports, and biographies. Joanne lives in New York State with her husband, three young daughters, and three crazy cats.